ALBERTA
THE BADLANDS

"Valley of the Moon", Deadlodge Canyon

ALBERTA
THE BADLANDS

Photographs by Brian Noble

Text by Glenn Rollans

A REIDMORE BOOK

Acknowledgements

We confess the obvious, that the effort of producing a book spills out of the authors' hands into the laps of innocent bystanders. We needed and appreciated all the assistance.

Thanks to Marna and Lynn, our families, Sid Andrews, Joseph Orosz, Hope Johnson, Robert Kroetsch, our publishers, the Film and Literary Arts Branch of Alberta Culture, and Alberta Recreation and Parks. There is a long list of others that we won't attempt to exhaust for fear of missing someone.

Many thanks.

Brian Noble and Glenn Rollans
Edmonton, 1981

Text © 1981 Glenn Rollans
Photographs © 1981 Brian Noble

CANADIAN CATALOGUING IN PUBLICATION DATA

Noble, Brian
Alberta, The Badlands
ISBN 0-919091-07-5

1. Alberta - Description and travel. - Views. 2. Drumheller region (Alta.). - Description and travel. - Views. I. Rollans, Glenn. II. Title.

FC 3695.D7N62 917.123'3 C81-091-297-X
F1079.D7N62

A Reidmore Book

Distributed in Canada by McClelland & Stewart Limited

Editorial	Randy Morse
Design	Randy Morse & Brian Noble
Preparation	Hallis Graphics Ltd.
Separations	Color Graphics Ltd.
Production	Randy Morse

Printed and bound in Canada

Dedication

We hope that this book will help you to recognize the remarkable in the ordinary, and the familiar in the bizarre.

B.N. & G.R.

Alkali pool, Milk River Badlands

Horseshoe Canyon, near Drumheller

Introduction

You anticipate the mountains for an hour, for two hours even, while approaching them. The far prospect, there on the horizon, swells from a cloud-like promise into dazzling novelty.

You have hardly a moment's notice when approaching the badlands. For a long while you are on the almost-rolling prairie, in fields of wheat and rape and grass, watching the neatness of fence and farmstead. Then the prairie abruptly yawns. There at the bumper's edge, at your feet, under your toes, is a dizzying emptiness. The eye lurches into a chasm.

To approach the badlands is to find a gap in the known and expected world. The surrounding prairie lulls you into a false sense of security, it fails to prepare you for this emptiness. Swinging off the highway to look at Horsethief Canyon, outside Drumheller, you at first doubt your own sense of space and time. You have come to the hollow and broken egg that gave birth to our dream of a dinosaur past.

Driving through the patches of thorny buffaloberry north-east from Brooks, past the last irrigation ditch and onto the reach of bald prairie, you come to an uneasy faltering of the horizon, as if the sky had somehow fallen into the earth. The horizon becomes, unimaginably almost, a receding vision of cliffs and buttes and mesas, as if the round earth had premonitions of its own end.

Geography has a secret motion, at once infinite and minute. I like to stop at the edge of the prairie to think for a while, to meditate, before descending into a badlands landscape. Entering the mountains one says hello. Entering the badlands, one somehow says good-by.

And the entrance into the badlands is so absolutely a descent. I suspect that for most of us, the experience is first of all visual. After the unimagined shapes of ribbed butte and capped hoodoo, one notices the horizontal layering, the grey-brown of clay and bentonite and ironstone that dissolves before one's eyes into purple and green and subtle hints of orange. Only later does one notice the bottom of the valley, the sagebrush flats, the sage like a cultivated crop, and then the more vivid green of the cottonwoods along the river.

I once entered the badlands of the Red Deer River by floating in on a boat. We spent a week, two friends and I, drifting in as the fossil hunters had drifted from Red Deer Crossing, during the first two decades of this century. What struck me on that entrance, on that series of entrances actually, was not so much sight as sound. We learned quickly to listen for a rapids. What we heard continually, endlessly, were the sounds of insects and birds. We heard the swishing waddle of a flock of nesting Canada geese. We heard the myriad cliff swallows, feeding around our ears it seemed. We listened for nighthawks and blue herons. The soundscape of the badlands is as rich and strange and exciting as the visual challenge.

It is the summer heat of the badlands that speaks to the visitor through the sense of touch. It was that heat that helped me understand the daily lives of the fossil hunters. I was writing a novel in which I invented an expedition that followed after the flatboats of Barnum Brown and Charles Hazelius Sternberg. I determined to prospect in the badlands until, on my own, I discovered the trace of a dinosaur skeleton.

After my friends and I pulled in our drifting boat at the Jenner Ferry, I went back into the badlands alone, spent three days walking and looking. I recommend such folly to no one. But I had the excuse that I was doing research, and I pushed myself, from sunrise to sunset. I learned to walk slowly, saving my strength and my water supply, under the burden of sun. I learned that the sudden sound of a grasshopper was not a rattlesnake, that antelope and deer can blur into a shimmering landscape that seems to offer no cover, that creeping juniper offers a secure foothold on a cliff's edge, that bunch grass sometimes conceals a quagmire of mud, that cushion cactus is painful to the hand. And when I found a chip of a dinosaur's bone, it was so absurdly visible, mounted on a little hoodoo of its own, that I was startled, almost frightened, by my own joyful laughter.

I understood, a little bit better, the eccentricity of the characters who entered the badlands and then could not leave, from the famous black rancher, John Ware, to Happy Jack the Ferryman.

I needed a rest. And I remembered the delightful couple, Mr. and Mrs. Leroux, who ran the hotel in Patricia, the last bed and the last meal and the last drink on the prairie's edge, above the badlands. I left my tent where I'd pitched it under a cottonwood and drove up out of Deadlodge Canyon.

I had stayed at the Patricia Hotel, during earlier visits to the badlands. I was from farther north in Alberta, I had grown up near the miniature badlands of the Battle River, and Mr. Leroux, understanding our various plagues, offered to trade me some snakes for some gophers.

He knew about my need to explore edges. He had once damned near drowned when he fell into an irrigation ditch, pursuing a pet goose that, in spite of its clipped wings, believed it could fly.

Mr. Leroux had three pet Canada geese. He could talk with them. I remember — I swear I was cold sober at the time — he led them into the bar, there in the Patricia Hotel. He had to wear one of those beaked prairie caps when he spoke to his geese. He put on his cap and opened the back door of the bar and in walked these three geese. They moved in perfect unison. Three beautiful, tall Canada geese, their heads turning, all together, this way and that, in the light of the bar. "Probably against the law," Mr. Leroux explained. Then he spoke goose to the geese and they all three, politely, left by the door through which they'd entered, went out into the darkness again.

A cowboy had been in the men's room during this brief visit. He came back into the bar, looked down at the calling card left on the floor by one of the geese, then stared up in disbelief at the ceiling. "Must've been flying low," he said. "For geese, that is."

The whole trick, in the badlands, is learning to deal with your own senses, your own perception and understanding. It takes years and years. It takes a lot of visits.

Robert Kroetsch

Badlands

Nature is a well that man can never fathom, an ocean with no shore. As long as men observe and think, they will be drawing water from well and ocean with no visible effect. The well will still be full and the shores remain unexplored.

Charles Hazelius Sternberg, fossil hunter, 1917

Milk River Canyon

Greasewood and rill formations

He was walking in the mauve blooms of bergamot, the radiant yellow of buffalo beans; he was loping through patches of wolf willow that rustled against his wet and dusty boots, the odour of sage rich and curative in his living nostrils.

Robert Kroetsch, Badlands, 1975

The four of us — Brian, Marna, Lynn and I — crammed into a Volkswagen Rabbit in the spring, and drove south for the badlands. It was a holiday weekend, so we avoided the main highway and headed south down a secondary road.

It was a bright, hot day. The dust devils twisted over ploughed fields, and the highway shifted under mirages and wavering heat. The grey fields smelled dry. The only relief was the deep black of freshly ploughed ground and the occasional flash of green on the side of a dugout or in a roadside ditch. We passed through farmland, then down into dry cattle country, counting pronghorn antelope as we went along. Finally we hit the road to Deadlodge Canyon, straight and dusty along the prairie.

Suddenly, we looked down into the badlands. We rolled along the level prairie, then the bottom fell out and the badlands were below us everywhere, filling our field of vision. Thousands upon thousands of hills, buttes, tables, seemed to stretch away forever. The road dropped into the valley, curled through a steep coulee. Abruptly, we were there.

The badlands towered on one side of us. On the other they formed a distant rim across the river, past the green border of cottonwoods along the water. Massive and monumental forms surrounded us.

We set up our tents in an old horse corral then walked out on the nearby sage flats. Evening was coming on, but the day was still clear and hot. As we approached the flats they looked like a meadow, steel-blue and soft, but when we stepped out into the sage we found that the ground was cracked mud which crunched under our feet.

Within a few steps, a cottontail rabbit shot away from under Lynn's feet. Had she stepped a foot farther away we would never have known it was there. Above us, in the hills, some people were climbing a scrub-covered knoll. Bits of conversation about jobs in Calgary drifted down to us, interrupted by the rustling sound of the dusk breeze in the dry brush and the quiet slapping of the river. In the low light, everything seemed coloured with the blue of the flat. An evergreen smell sharpened the air as we walked toward the river border of cotton-woods, through clumps of chokecherry, patches of snowberry, and thickets of willow brush.

We stopped near an old cottonwood and plucked a few leaves of sage, rubbed them together between our fingers, and held the pulp to our noses. The smell was slightly bitter, slightly sour, a mixture of juniper and spruce. The lone tree which rose above us seemed immensely old. Dead wood was mixed with the live; green limbs grew from a hollow and blackening trunk.

A little farther on, we scared a pintail off her eggs. She had nested in the grass, hundreds of yards away from the nearest water. All around her, rippled, dry gutters showed where water once had flowed when she nested. Now, in the early spring, the mud was already curling like leaves in the fall. The duck flew around us, squawking and quacking, in a low, even circle. We left the nest and watched to see when she would land, but her patience outlasted ours.

Badlands stood like galleries around us. We walked a bit further, climbed a sharp-sided hill, and sat on the fractured rock at its edge with our faces to the breeze. The evening was cooling. We batted at the mosquitoes, looked down over the river, across the badlands, and listened for the broken whisper of voices.

We decided to take a short loop through the hills before heading back to our sleeping bags. Outlines were softening in the dusk; the landscape was becoming deceptive. A channelled hillside just out of arm's reach seemed to be miles away. It was a perfect cliff face; the detail, the contours of the rock and the scale told our eyes they were looking at something distant and enormous. Its water patterns and strata were too complex, too perfect, to be as small as in fact they were.

We climbed and descended like ants on a gravel road: through gullies, down wash-outs, over hillocks, and across level white tables. As we climbed and descended, the temperature of the air around us changed. On a low rise, the air was warm, but a step or two took us into a cool hollow. Every moment of increasing darkness made daytime detail invisible while bringing some new feature into view. The dusk proceeded in gentle, distant stages.

The temperature fell, notch by notch, and the mosquitoes retired. The bats came out and flitted around our heads. For some reason they followed us as we walked back toward our camp. The air was still extremely clear. The stars emerged, the evening breeze calmed; night was quiet.

We filled up our water containers, put on sunscreen, and headed down little Sandhill Creek the next morning.

We stayed out through the heat of the day. There was almost no shade; the rounded hillsides gave the sun a clear path to the valley bottom. The ground and the air were dry; our sweat disappeared before we felt it. The stream beds that cut across the valley bottom were empty. Here and there a little remaining mud trapped spread-eagled moths and butterflies, and in spots, enough moisture remained to grow some green grass. Over most of the area, nothing grew on the dry ground except greasewood, prickly-pear cactus, and the odd tuft of grass browning in the sun.

Looking across the badlands from the hilltops, we felt breezes that missed the valley floor. The air was clear and outlines were sharp. Colours were distinct, but hot and bleached: endless variations on red, brown, yellow, and grey. The hillsides around us displayed their strata with rain-washed clarity. Every hillock and mound declared that the land's substrate had been built in layers.

At the foot of these hills, we walked across glaring, white, cement-like pediments. These flat borders at the bases of badlands hills are paved by fine clays that wash down from above. We found fossil material on most, mixed with other bits of sedimentary debris. The evidence of environmental change was laid out on the hard tables: clam shells, fragments of tortoise shells, the plated skins of crocodillians, and pieces of large dinosaur limb bones. The fragments stood on small pedestals; water had washed away the fine clays around them.

We were picking our way across a steep hillside, looking down into sinkholes where water had dissolved a path to subterranean passages, when a mule deer came over the crest of the hill perhaps fifty feet from us, and snorted in surprise. It turned and spronged off down the slope, all four of its legs leaving the ground at each bound, picking up speed with perfect control. We moved much more cautiously, yet still ended up with cactus spines driven through our shoe soles.

We hadn't seen a square foot of land that day that didn't show evidence of water action, but we had seen almost no *water* at all. The pediments surfaced with water-washed clays, the stream and rivulet beds that cut across the valley, and the hills themselves were all water-carved features, but they were all desert-dry. When we came down from the hillside and found an actual pool of water, it was startling.

The pool was perhaps four feet deep, fed by a trickling waterfall that seemed to come from nowhere. Except for ripples radiating from the splashing of the tiny rivulet, it was completely calm. Water racers skittered across it and cast large round shadows with their feet.

We walked a great deal during the morning. Often sedimentary debris covered the slopes and made it hard to get a firm footing. The walking, though, took us to gentler spots. We climbed to a rounded grassy hilltop where the wind could be felt, and were presented on one side with an unusual view of a rock face, and on the other with a sweep of apparently endless badlands, cloud shadows moving across them to the southeast. The cliff was as deceptive as the small hill had been the night before. Perspective in the badlands is confused and confusing; this formation was no more than two hundred yards away, but it appeared to be a towering canyon wall seen from a distance of miles. Its strata showed clearly.

Strata record the history of the badlands, the particular deposition of water-carried sediments that formed this erodable area. We were looking at a cross section of a geological formation called the "Oldman" which was laid down seventy-five to eighty million years ago during the Upper Cretaceous period.

In Alberta, the Cretaceous was a time of change in surface features. This area had been on the margin of a great inland sea, where sediments slowly built up in the marshes and backwaters, and on the deltas and floodplains. The rock wall we faced showed the sediments distinctly: clays, sandstones, siltstones and mudstones. The colours were stacked grey upon brown upon grey upon black.

Even with the breeze, we were all uncomfortable in the blaze of the afternoon. We tried to find cool spots, but there weren't many. Finally we headed for Little Sandhill Creek, a narrow band of green that flowed through the valley. It ran waist deep in places, bordered with cottonwoods and fresh green grass, sectioned by beaver dams. We rushed to pull off our shoes and socks and splashed into the welcome cool of the creek. We picked our way over the rough bottom, skirted patches of quick-mud, and waded through old beaver ponds. We stayed in this wet, green corridor for the entire walk back to the campground.

A deer trail paralleled the stream, through the scrub, under cottonwoods, and through patches of brilliant yellow buffalobean. At some points, we could look up and see cars moving along a road on the prairie rim above. A few people watched us from the roadside. During the entire day, we had not been more than a couple of miles from the road, yet we hadn't seen a sign of a human from the time we stepped into the badlands.

April   6 Tues.   16° *above First Crows and Robins*
       7 Wed.   14° *above First Ducks*
       8 Thurs. 28° *above Ice Moved a Little*
       9 Fri.   30° *above Plowed some*
      11 Sun. 22° *above Snow*
      12 Mon. 6° *above Dam Sunny Alberta*

"Happy Jack" Jackson in his Diary, 1909

Cottonwood, evening

Prairie Crocus, valley grasslands

Decaying cottonwood and shrubs

Glacial erratic, Little Sandhill Creek

Prickly Pear cactus and Oldman sediments

Glacial rock and lichen

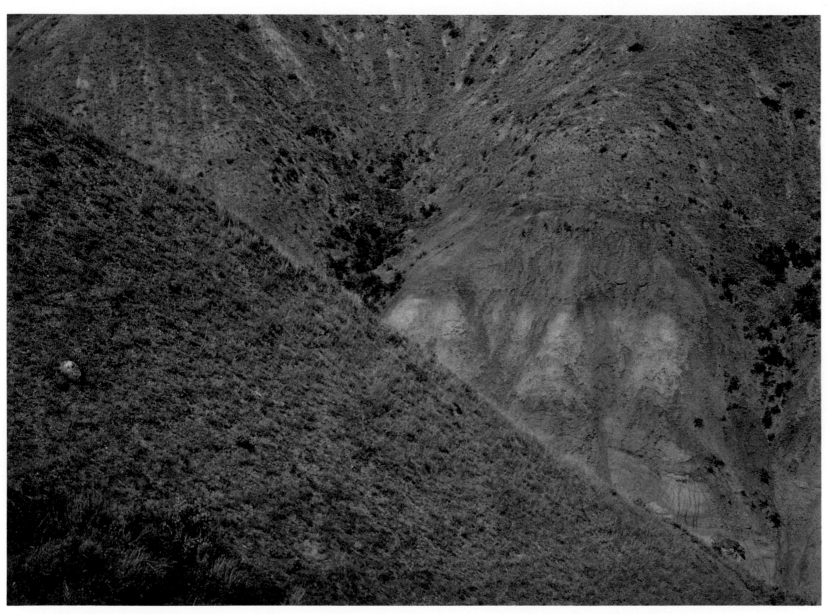

Little Sandhill Creek Canyon

Cutbank and Steveville Badlands

Departed Ghostpine late morning, the valley a mile wide here, the Badlands 400 feet deep, ridged, pinnacled, some of the buttes cut down to tables, the tableland cut down to sugarloafs and knolls. And up above us on the high plains, open prairie now, the wind blowing. A dry prairie wind comes scorching down into the valley.

The character William Dawe in Badlands by Robert Kroetsch

It was only the middle of May, but the days were long and hot, and the Red Deer was already a sluggish, muddy stream. We decided the next morning to wade the river and explore the badlands on the north bank. When we squished up through the mud on the far side, we found that we had to struggle through a hundred yards of thorny brush under the cottonwoods before emerging.

The areas of vegetation that dot the riverbank as a green series of oases in an otherwise dry and treeless area are the Riparian habitat. Plains cottonwoods stand over a tangle of brush, willows, snowberry, thorny buffaloberry and wild rose.

We had seen cattle standing here the night before, bellowing out across the river, but they were gone now. The trees shelter deer and cattle and are also the home of badlands nesting birds — herons, hawks and songbirds — and a roosting place for the great-horned owl. We pressed on at the expense of scratches and scrapes.

Once through, we climbed into the badlands. When we decided to rest, we were forced to protect ourselves from the blazing sun with shirts and sunscreen, the only barriers we could put between our skin and the sky.

From the hilltop we paused on, we could see a great curve of the Red Deer, rimmed by prairie and badlands. People were splashing around on a sandbar, a mile or two downstream. The day was so still that, even from that distance, we could hear the shouts of children.

Brian retained more energy than the rest of us. With him leading the way, we came upon a row of hoodoos standing just above the grass flat that led down to the cottonwoods. Hoodoos are the cliches of the badlands; you can't describe them without saying that they stand like mushrooms or sentinels, because that is exactly how they stand.

Huge flat capstones were lying about on the ground. Next to them, tall slender hoodoos seemed ready to topple, and beside those stood the youngest hoodoos, still thick and strong. A hoodoo is formed when a piece of fairly strong rock is located above a layer of eroding softer rock. The stronger rock partially protects the material beneath it from water erosion. The result is a tablet of rock standing on a thin, fluted pillar. Built by erosion, hoodoos are transitory features on a badlands landscape. A capstone can protect its pedestal for only so long before runoff topples the formation.

We sat beneath them in the shade and rested our backs against the smooth columns. Despite the fact that we realized that many years of slow weathering had produced these structures, and that their stability had allowed them to stand while their surroundings were scraped away, we all half-worried that the precarious-looking capstones would pick that moment to collapse on us. We shouldn't have been concerned; hoodoos fall only when there is no one around to see or hear.

Lightning broke in and from the sky, lacing the clouds, the clouds like precious china for an instant fractured and broken, the perfection of dark blue laced with the lesions of light. The thunder came distant, ominous. It rolled and faded.

Robert Kroetsch, Badlands

The nighthawks came out in the early evening. They climbed into the quiet sky with three beats of their slender, tapered wings. A squawk, another three beats, a cry and then a dive, cutting the air with vibrating feathers, producing a half-moan of wind on wings, a low *whoom*.

We clawed our way up a steep clay slope onto a hilltop, then faced the river to the north. A storm front was swelling on the horizon, two-armed and threatening. As we stood and looked out over the valley through a light evening haze, the clouds began to split as if to flow around us on both sides, flicking bursts of lightning to the prairie below. When the strikes were especially violent, we heard and felt a soft, low physical wave of thunder.

We decided to risk staying so Brian could photograph the storm. While he set up his equipment, I had a look around for the easiest way down from our exposed perch. Just in case. When bentonitic clays get wet, they swell to two or three times their dry volume. Their crumbly surface becomes smooth and slick, the ground feels greased; every step taken risks a slip. Attempting a wet hillside after a rain usually results in a rough ride to the valley bottom.

There was no easy way off. We were standing on a steep-sided, dry badlands island, and all the banks were clay. The storm's outriders began to close around us, but still we stayed.

"It's going to go around us," said Brian, taking pictures. "I don't think we'll get the lightning." He sounded more hopeful than certain.

The wind began to pick up. In a moment the rain was pelting down. Through the downpour, a rainbow appeared on the edge of the storm over the prairie. I huddled down to stay as dry as I could while huge drops splattered me with grit.

The rain turned to hail, marble-sized and painful, and with it came a simultaneous flash and clap as lightning struck somewhere very close. The next strike was so near it sounded — it *felt* — like sand ground between my teeth. Brian looked at his steel tripod as if he was noticing it for the first time, then threw it hastily away. We exchanged quick, nervous smiles.

Water was now coursing down the networks of rills and runnels, feeding into a shallow ditch. We jumped into it and got as low as we could. The thunder shook us again, mixed rain and hail fell in scouring sheets, but the heart of the storm was past. Thick silty water flowed along our ditch, then down every crevice in the hillside. The rainbow to the north now stretched over the prairie in a complete arc.

A moment later, the rain and hail stopped, but the sound of water continued. Water rushed downward, heavy and dark, sweeping along gullies that had been bone dry when we walked up them an hour earlier. Now they were noisy with silt-laden water. We stood, dripping and hail-beaten, hearts thumping, and watched the storm move on.

The clouds were strangely elongated as they moved away from us. They looked as if they were being sucked through a small opening directly over the valley; they bunched and whirled at the entrance.

After another search, we found a spot on the hillside that was dotted with tufts of grass. These had stabilized the clay enough to form small steps as the hillside eroded away. By the time we had slowly picked our way down the slope, the sound of water had almost ceased. The clays were already drying in the late evening sun.

The entire experience — abrupt, tremendously exciting, and unrecommended — was over. The nighthawks were back in the air. Their sounds, mixed with the slap of our feet on the wet valley floor, were soon all we could hear.

On a summer afternoon near Little Sandhill Creek, the only shade was under the cottonwoods near the river's edge, which was where swarms of mosquitoes spent their time, too. We decided to follow a trail near our campsite, trading off the bugs for the direct light of the sun.

We walked slowly through the sage, looking for bullsnakes, but they avoided our company. The day was remarkably still. White areas of the eroded landscape around us glared transparently; the greys were white, the browns were grey. The miniaturized, rugged ranges that lay around us confused our sense of scale. Tiny cloud-shadows sped across the landscape, fanned by breezes that didn't touch us at all.

We crossed successions of stream beds. The swirling clay patterns on their bottoms mimicked the flow of water, but now the streams were dry. Nearby, a buck lay under an overhanging rock ledge in a scrap of shade.

I stood watching him from the opposite, north-facing slope. In sun-beaten, eroded terrain such as this, the north-facing slopes receive what little mercy nature offers. The sun's rays strike them at a reduced angle, and as a result, they sometimes retain enough water to support relatively lush vegetation. This slope was on the edge of greenery. It was covered in juniper and grass, sprinkled with bluebells, daisies, and here and there a patch of sweet clover. The deer, though, had the only shade. He lay watching me with big, deep eyes and alert ears. I walked away from him, hoping to hear the boom of his feet as he vacated the hollow, but he obviously valued the cool spot more than he worried about me. He didn't move.

A few steps further on, I passed a bare sandstone ridge. It was humped and long like the back of a sleeping bull, its sides streaked with thin lines of light rose. Along its top, coral-coloured sediments had eroded out in thin, symmetrical rings. Between the rings the sandstone had a blue tinge; around the base of the ridge were fragments of ironstone coated in black magnesium dioxide. Brian caught up with me and pointed out the crumbling clay and ironstone debris that marked levee sands, sediments that once settled from slow water on the banks of an ancient river.

The intricate bedding in the ridge showed the calm that had covered this spot millions of years ago; the calm of still waters depositing fine particles in even layers. Those days could have been no stiller than this one. We were moving while the deer, the jackrabbits, and even the bullsnakes had the sense to lie still.

We drove out to Steveville the next evening, down dusty side roads, past a natural gas pumping station, then by old windbreaks that were yielding to a new, wilder growth of trees. We stopped at a farmhouse in a bare yard overlooking the valley, where a man and woman stood trying to link up sections of a self-propelled irrigator. Brian got out of the car and hailed them; when they looked toward us the sections fell apart again. They said we could head into the badlands below the house, so we turned down the little-used road that dropped away from the prairie.

The undercarriage of the car bruised and tore the vegetation between the road ruts; the scent of sage filled the vehicle. We followed an old road grade as it crossed into the valley. Water had pockmarked its surface with sinkholes. We picked our way around them until we came to a large mudhole that blocked our path.

The grade was bentonitic clay here, the same clay shaped by "popcorn erosion" that lined the hillsides around us. The clays, composed mostly of volcanic ash, form dry, hard, crumbly knobs that texture the slopes. In the middle of the road grade, water had collected and soaked the bentonite, turning it from grey to mocha, pudding-heavy and greasy to the touch. The hole was grown over by rushes that somehow wrested the mositure they needed from the viscous mud.

We continued on foot. Small hills and ridges, ten or twenty feet high, covered the area. The ground seemed covered more in fossils than dust. The mounds displayed cross-bedding of fine silts and clays; the place had been a backwater or swamp when the bone remains collected.

We poked around with our faces close to the ground, picking out crocodillian teeth and other small bones, until it began to get dark. As the sun set, a blanket of heavy cloud rolled across the sky, hiding the slow emergence of the stars. Several nighthawks and a single prairie falcon climbed and dove nearby as we walked back. The falcon was hunting something on the ground. In comparison with the nighthawks, its climbs were higher, its dives sleeker. It was silent except for its harsh call; its wings cut the air cleanly.

As we drove back to our camp, the cloud cover retreated to reveal the night sky, bareness broken by bright spots and striking patterns, empty spaces highlighting scattered bits of beauty, and a great sweep of slowly-changing forms.

I took a walk in the moonless dark. The only sounds were the flit of bats around my head, the frogs and the crickets. When I stopped to listen to the quiet, the mosquitoes caught up and whined in my ears, so I moved on and returned to camp. As I slipped off to sleep, the wind came up, a dry breeze that kept the sky swept clear.

All this region, except of course the river channel and flood plain, was transformed by nature's sculptury into fantastic badland scenery, the rocks carved into the most intricate patterns, entirely devoid of vegetation, except, perhaps, along the northern slope of some rounded bluff, where sponge-moss had secured a precarious foothold; while running through it were trailing junipers, and spruces, with flowers of many a hue (to delight the eye) after searching the steep and barren slopes for hours.

Charles H. Sternberg

Hoodoos, Mexico Ranch Badlands

Hoodoo formations, Deadlodge Canyon

Hoodoo

Greasewood and sagebrush on swollen clays

Intermittent waterfall

Thunderhead, Munson

Evening, Steveville Badlands

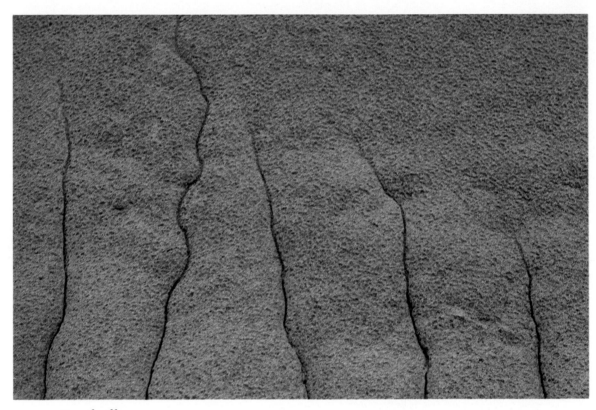

Pencil rills

"Popcorn" erosion, "Bentonite" clay

Mule deer, Little Sandhill Creek

Evening, Milk River Canyon

Evening, Pinhorn Grasslands

Nature has a wonderful work shop for the Creator, one continual plant, for turning out perfect living forms endowed with life and power.

Charles H. Sternberg

As the earth tilted toward the summer solstice, we drove south through Lethbridge in the sweeping, grassy valley of the Oldman, on our way to the Milk River Badlands. We stopped in the town of Milk River in the faded, dusty, early evening for gas and water. We had a long way to go before stopping for the night.

The day was still cruelly hot as we drove past irrigated farmland and dry ranchland. Navigating with survey maps, we took the Aden turnoff and started south. Ahead of us loomed the Sweetgrass Hills, just across the border in Montana. The evenings were long at this time of the year; it was nine o'clock and still broad daylight.

We turned onto a little-used road on the south side of the Milk River, and followed it as it deteriorated from gravel to large cobbles to rock to dirt to grass. We were all anxious to stop for the evening, as the Sweetgrass Hills purpled steadily, commanding the prairie, monumental and symmetric. We followed the grass track as far as we could, but eventually the road crossed a stream bed with walls too sharp and high for the car. We stopped in the middle of grazing cattle. In the summer they wander far into the leased grazing lands. Now they lurched up around the car, stupidly curious. We mooed back at them.

We set up camp on top of a little rise on the bald prairie. We could see neither river nor valley, but according to our map both were near us to the north. We started toward them, walking away the monotony of the cramped drive, through the deepening evening. As we walked we scared up a dozen Canada geese from a marshy spot to the northwest. They lumbered into the air, honking. A kestrel hovered above us. The sound of nighthawks diving carried to us even when the birds were too far away to be seen; their swooping hum is as characteristic of the summer prairie as the yelps of coyotes.

The mourning doves were also beginning to call as we set out. Horned larks flitted across the grass, low stubby little darting figures. We passed long-billed curlews and avocets in a wet depression. An ominous-looking thunderhead seemed to be settling on us from the north, reaching out, flattening against the prairie.

Farther ahead in a soft-sided dry gully, we suddenly came upon an antelope, then another and another. About twenty of the slender, short pronghorns showed themselves, snorting and blowing a bit. They watched us intently and wandered closer, not quite sure what we were. We stood still, surprised and amused and watched while the main body stopped and a couple of males came ahead on their own. They rounded a bend in the gully and were on top of us, then stopped short, seeing we weren't antelope. Startled, they sprang back to the rest of the group. By the time they rejoined the others they had recovered their composure, so they stood and watched us for a moment before turning to haughtily lead an orderly retreat.

We started back to camp as it began to get really dark. Coyotes were barking and the nighthawks and doves contributed their melancholy sounds. The thunderhead had dissipated; it looked as if we were to be spared rain. We could see a tiny light across the border in the Sweetgrass Hills, and the cattle were making evening noises nearby. It was as if we stood on a pole with the earth spinning around us; this spot was lonely and powerful. We climbed into the warmth of our sleeping bags as the night soothed the coyotes and birds into silence.

We slept the morning after our first night on the prairie until it grew hot enough to make our sleeping bags uncomfortable. After some breakfast, we hiked into the badlands. As we entered along a gently sloping coulee, we could see that the valley was extremely deep, the hills tall and rust-coloured. The Milk River was still hidden. The hilltops ahead were littered with fractured red sedimentary rock; the slopes were steep and grassy. Flowers were out: a pink blossom we couldn't identify, pretty purple vetches and bluebells.

A little draw dotted with pools of clear water led us down into the badlands. We splashed our faces, which were already sticky with sweat in the early morning, and disturbed the clay in the water so that murky clouds rose and spread.

At the base of this draw was a dry stream bed, roughened by angular rocks which were propped and piled on each other. We assumed that following this water course would quickly lead us to the river. As the creek swept down through the hills, the slopes rose steeply on either side to a great height. It became a bit claustrophobic as we went further down. Each step put that much more effort between us and a return to the prairie, but the strongest pull was toward the river. We picked our way over large piles of jumbled rocks. The slabs balanced one upon another; they tipped away under our feet.

Every so often we considered leaving the stream bed to follow a tributary gully, but decided against it and kept to our course. The end of the trail came suddenly when the bed of the creek suddenly droped off perpendicularly to a mass of broken rock. We had no choice now but to go up. The gentlest slope nearby was a hundred and fifty vertical feet at an angle of fity degrees, made tricky by unavoidable patches of scree.

Three-quarters of the way up we were arrested by a large cluster of prickly-pear cactus flowers. They were a brilliant, glossy yellow, ringed inside with greenish or bluish stamens that were crawling with insects. As the bugs moved or as we brushed the stamens with our fingertips, the straw-like structures moved of their own force toward the centre of the blossom, toward the pistil.

Lynn finally went ahead and found a feasible route for completing the climb. We followed and came to a grassy hilltop. The view was astounding, a composite of everything we had seen from below. Ponderous, steeply-walled hills surrounded us. The colours were strong: deep iron-red rock crumbling on the hilltops, golden grass, brown slashes, hot bluish clay, and far off, far below, the Milk River, a tiny trickle meandering back and forth, around and back again lined with green cottonwoods and brush. We had been nowhere near the river when we were forced to leave the gully; the badlands went on and on.

Behind us was the prairie, but between us and it were what seemed to be countless ridges and valleys. We set off along a narrow, grassy ridge toward a cluster of hoodoos overlooking a steep valley. The capstones were enormous and flat, sitting on broad bases. We climbed onto one. The sun was still shining hotly, but we caught the brunt of a cold, sweeping wind and were soon shivering, although our skin felt hot to the touch.

We continued along the base of the ridge, where Lynn found a badly fragmented fossil dinosaur tooth in the bentonitic clay, the tooth of a large carnivore. I looked around hoping to repeat her find, and discovered an arrowhead of the Oxbow type. It had a bright white patina that made it stand out from the litter of pebbles in which it lay near the dinosaur tooth. It was the first trace of people that we had seen.

From the ridge, we stepped into a broad, shallow basin, interrupted by small mounds of clay and small bentonite pits filled with bits of fossilized clam shell. The white ground bounced the sun back at us like a reflector oven.

We sat and baked a while, letting the warmth ease our aches, then stepped onto the prairie. We were soon discovered by a couple of mule deer that came trotting toward us, obviously pleased to see fellow deer, until they got a better look. Like the antelope, they stopped short with a snort, sprang around and bounded off with more indignation than fear.

We faced the Sweetgrass Hills as we walked. The three main peaks clustered together solidly, stonily, rising with volcanic suddeness above their surroundings. The prairie centred on these hills; they seemed both tyrant and protector.

That evening, we ate under a hovering kestrel. As the light began to soften, Brian and Marna took their flashlights and started back toward the badlands to see them in their evening colours. Lynn and I stayed behind to light the lantern when it got dark.

An antelope grazed nearby; it circled us slowly, lifting its head and watching us every so often. From time to time it uttered an odd loud noise, something between a trumpet and a cough. It stayed at a safe distance. We were definitely intruding.

The prairie cooled so quickly that we soon had our sweaters pulled over our sunburns. We lit the lantern and eventually saw two unsteady lights coming toward us. The luxurious silence again grew as the temperature dropped. We had the prairie to ourselves for another night.

The next morning rolled back out along the dusty roads we had come in on. By eight, the day was already astoundingly hot. Before the town of Milk River, we turned on the road leading to Writing-on-Stone Park.

We set up camp, and found a path in the hoodoos above the campground that took us east out of the park.

It was difficult walking through the hoodoos, but it was nice to have the twisting, quiet river below us, bordered in places by a cottonwood margin. Around us was a fantastic circus of rock, a forest of hoodoos. Every cool hollow seemed to hold a cottontail rabbit that would rather take its chances on being caught by the ears than leave the shade.

We rested for a while on the side of a gully. When we moved on, we crossed above a silent ranchhouse and saw a cool peninsula below us. It was covered in tall old trees and ringed off almost entirley by the meandering river. We headed toward it along the raccoon-tracked mud bank beside the river. A ring-necked pheasant rocketed squawking across our path.

Once across the mud and through the brush, we found a refuge under the cottonwoods. It was shaded, furnished with beaver-cut benches, and enveloped in a quiet that demanded relaxed reflection. The noise of the shallow Milk River washing by the bank, cutting into the peninsula, was the only sound I cared to hear just then; it spoke of coolness, and leisure.

The day was wearing on, so we left the place sooner than I wanted to and walked back quickly through the hoodoos to our camp.

Lynn, who had stayed behind, told us that she had come upon a rattlesnake sunning itself; both she and the snake survived. We pulled down our tents and loaded up, tried to wash some of the grime off, then got into the car and climbed out of the valley. Marna wanted a Coors, so over my protests at the long drive ahead, we headed for the Aden border crossing.

After passing the Canadian Customs office, a neat trailer with a uniformed young woman inside, we pulled up to the American station. The officer, working on a tractor out back, came up wiping his hands on his pants. Brian asked him where the nearest Coors was to be found. "Thirty miles", he said, "and then no guarantee." We turned back to Canada without the beer.

We passed through the town of Milk River taking turns sucking on a jug of warm water. We were already hot, tired and thirsty, with seven or eight hours of driving ahead of us. The ride home was broken only by a fly-ridden dinner. I accidentally set a picnic table on fire and Brian spilled our spaghetti all over the ground. The badlands had taken a lot out of us.

Sandstone blocks, Milk River Badlands

Prickly Pear cactus flower

Water in dry stream bed

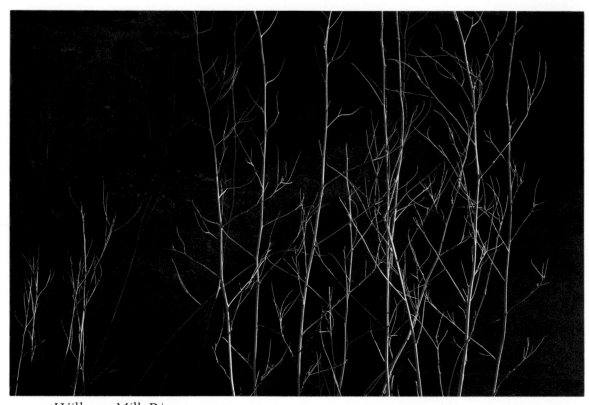

Willows, Milk River

Writing-on-Stone and Sweetgrass Hills

Milk River Valley

Wild Rose and sandstone

Badlanders

Requires a special breed of man. A brave man. A fool. An adventurer who can endure the boredom of flies and heat. Searching all day in vain. Digging a grave to get the corpse out.

William Dawe in Badlands by Robert Kroetsch

Buttes, Munson Badlands

Fossil wood

So we searched over miles and miles of badlands, week after week. I was completely exhausted at night, after a day's unsuccessful hunt. There is no work so trying, as that of clinging hour after hour to steep ascents, and searching every inch of exposed surface, in and out among the winding slopes.

Charles H. Sternberg

We pulled up the canoe near One Tree Creek early in the day. The sun was already hot as we walked through the willows to the dry valley floor. Brian and I took turns carrying our pack with the water in it. The jug had a slow leak, so the water carrier had the benefit of a cool, wet back.

Brian was leading me to some fossil sites. He'd been here before, climbing down from the prairie, but it was the first time either of us had arrived by water. There are many stories connected with the river route into these badlands. People who know this area know of its fossils, and people who know about the fossils usually know stories about fossil hunters. The early bone prospectors, latter-day pioneers whose frontier was time, learned that the easiest way in and out of badlands, especially when moving tons of fossil and rock, was by river.

We saw a great deal of fossil material as we walked along: fragments of tortoise shell, dermal scutes of crocodillians, bits of bone and pieces of marine shell. Here and there we came across large pieces of limb bone scattered down rills in the hillsides that lay ahead of us in an intricate, wavering jumble. Brian enjoyed the scenery at ground level, the pieces of bone, and identified fragments for me. His enthusiasm was contagious; I was soon fighting off the urge to collect, knowing the laws against amateur removal of fossils.

The concentration of fossil reptiles along the valley was what attracted a steady trickle of bone hunters from 1873 on. The early collectors — Dawson, Tyrell, Weston, Lamb — were intrigued by the dinosuar remains, but they had problems collecting successfully. An Alberta farmer visiting the American Museum of Natural History in New York in 1909 mentioned the bones he had seen back home to Barnum Brown, a paleontologist at the Museum. Soon the real dinosaur rush was on. Brown had extensive experience in collecting fossils, and he was the first to collect in this valley with practiced success.

Brown had come down the same stretch of river we had, but he had travelled on a heavy freight raft rather than in a canoe. We had been having trouble keeping our light craft in the slow river's main channel; the effort for Brown's group must have been considerably greater. Even the walking we were doing now in the shadeless valley was exhausting. Digging out, preparing and moving huge chunks of fossil and rock must have required enormous endurance —and they had to *find* the fossils first.

Successive hilltops gave us ever-changing views of ranks of hills, layered with sediments, glaring in the sun. It was hard to imagine the conditions in which dinosaurs had lived here. Near the end of the Cretaceous period, approximately seventy-five million years ago, this spot was part of a broad coastal plain. It was lush, hot and humid, a series of deltas, ponds and swamps, something like the present-day Mississippi delta. Steadily evolving generations of reptiles, from enormous herbivores to ostrich-sized bird-mimics, lived and died during an age that lasted at least twenty times longer than man in any form has been on earth.

Late in the day, we began looking for a fossil quarry site that was marked on our map. Brown came back to the Red Deer Valley for five successive seasons, helping the American Museum to build what was probably the world's best collection of Upper Cretaceous dinosaurs. He and other collectors then and since have taken hundreds of specimens from the valley. Quarry sites are sprinkled throughout the badlands; even seventy years of rapid erosion haven't hidden the early digs.

We couldn't find the site, but in looking for it Brian found the weathered skeleton of a duckbilled dinosaur. The bones were badly fragmented but lying in place. Water-cuts dissected the skeleton, but if you stood back and crossed the gaps with your imagination, you could see a form stretching twenty-five feet. The shoulder and hipbone were brown, sandy patches of tiny fragments; the vertebrae were exposed as a connect-the-dots spine. Two or three years earlier it might have been a good find, but dinosaur hunting is a matter of being in the right place at the right time. Water does the digging, at least at first, but the fossils erode almost as fast as the hillsides.

Brian also found a post lying on the dry hilltop, a mile or so from the river. Obviously beaver-cut on one end, it was the kind of pole that a fossil hunter could have used as a lever or roller. It wasn't unreasonable to make that connection. Every bit of debris, like the pole, tells a story of a specific intrusion; things remain where they are left. Recent history and the history of things long past — remains of fossil hunting and fossils — lie in such close association in the badlands that the passage of time seems unimportant.

In fact, though, change is constant. As we set up for the night, a light rain began to fall, and even as we watched, a layer of the hills began to flow toward the river.

We see spread out upon our board
The canned food that our mess afford.
The sickening beans and peas galore
We've feasted on so oft before;

The pail of water standing there
Is Alkali. My friends, beware!
"Hash is ready," our cook cries,
And we sit down to fight off flies.

From "A Story of the Past," Charles H. Sternberg, 1911

We walked back into the badlands near One Tree Creek the next morning. It was still a bit hazy; tatters of mist were being torn back from the hills as the sun warmed up. The hillsides were damp and dark, the strata stood out like the grain in oiled wood.

The scenes we saw were the same recorded by one of the first photographers in these badlands: George Sternberg. He first saw these hills in the summer of 1913 while part of a fossil-hunting team led by his father, Charles H. Sternberg. George's brothers Levi and Charlie were also part of the team. The four Sternbergs had been engaged by the Geological Survey of Canada to compete with Barnum Brown, to collect fossils before Brown found and removed them. Noises had been made in Ottawa because of the export of this Canadian resource.

Brian had brought along copies of some of George's photographs: shots of fossil digs with long panoramas of the valley in the background. Using the photographs and our map, we found some of the old quarry sites. Sticks and logs visible in the photographs lay weathered but undistrubed. While erosion had softened some contours, the lines of the valley were largely unchanged.

The association of the Sternbergs with the valley lasted for decades. Charles Hazelius Sternberg sired a line of single-minded fossil hunters. He was the son of a Kansas preacher, and he searched out the fossil record with religious enthusiasm. He didn't bring his sons here for the scenery or the wilderness experience; isolation and arduous work in this fantastic landscape came with the job. He was a compulsive fossil-finder, and his devotion to the search, the effort to understand the past was unswerving. A son, Charlie, was still finding and preparing fossils in Alberta's badlands until the 1960s.

Alberta was a perfect area for dinosaurs during the Upper Cretaceous, and here lay the proof. At that time, this area was the fringe of an inland sea where the same conditions that supported dinosaurs also permitted their preservation and fossilization. Corpses settled into silty bottoms or were washed into backwaters. Sediments were deposited over them, beginning the slow process of mineralization.

Sedimentation continued long after the dinosaurs were gone, but glaciation scraped away some of the accumulated overburden from the fossil-bearing strata. Then water cut into the remaining deposits. Water flowing down the valley, and into the valley from the surrounding plains, steadily carried away some of the sands and silts that surrounded the fossils, preparing the site for the Sternbergs.

As the day warmed, it was clear that erosion hadn't done all the work. Prowling the hills systematically for fossils must have been at times disheartening work. Where the clay was wet, we fought to keep from skating, and where it was dry, we skidded on the scree.

Having watched the brown, muddy rain runoff the night before, it was hard to believe that anything could last a year in these badlands, yet it had taken the fossils here *seventy thousand millenia* to emerge. It was an odd crossing of paths that put men like the Sternbergs here at precisely the right moment in geological history. Following their tracks emphasized the enormous span of time displayed in the hills and sharp-cut gullies, the flats and buttes all around us. We stood at the tip of an immense pyramid of history, dwarfed by the mass of events below us, without even the distinction of being the first to stand on that precarious spot.

It was time to find a place to spend the night, so we reluctantly moved on. We hiked back out to the canoe, pushed off, and headed down-river.

Left at Mr. M.J. Stapleton's Jenner P.O. Alta.
Left three horses (2 geldings & one mare)
One set harness. One Great West Saddle,
one bridle Two spurs Two picket ropes
& picket pines
One old tent, 9 × 9, Three sets tent poles,
one old stove & pipe one Milk can.
One mess box with dishes and cooking utensils.
Two axes, One water bag
One pair old rubber boots.
Charles H. Sternberg in his field notes, September 25, 1915

February	17 Thurs.	Coldest Day 36° Below
	22 Tues.	42° Below
	27 Sat.	Chinook 42° above
July	8 Fri.	Dry Dry Dam Dry
	16 Sat.	God Knows & Directs all Things for the Best amen
	17 Sun.	106° in The Shade
	18 Mon.	Pretty Close to Hell
	19 Tues.	Big Foot Had a Cat
	24 Sun.	No Need of Elevators for Grain This Year

God Damed Hot & Dry

"Happy Jack" Jackson, 1910

We pulled the canoe up on a pebble bar in the middle of a fall day. We were at an old ferry crossing, across from Wolf Coulee, downstream from Deadlodge Canyon. An old road grade snaked down to the water's edge on the other side of the river.

Brian and I had both been anxious to get to this spot all day. The ferry had been run by a badlands original: Happy Jack Jackson. Most people near this stretch of river know his story, but the actual setting is so inaccessible that few have seen it. We walked up the bank into a stand of big cottonwoods. They were turning colour; the green of their leaves was mixed with a blazing auburn.

The mosquitoes along the bank didn't seem to realize that it was fall, but as we walked up through the trees we got away from the worst of them. We passed through a border of willows, and there stood Happy Jack's ranch.

It was actually a collection of buildings: stables, a workshop, and three tiny cabins huddled together. The buildings sat on a bare sage flat, the least-sheltered spot around. With badlands as a backdrop and the shelter of the cottonwoods several hundred yards away, the buildings looked defiantly exposed.

The rancher and ferryman's proper name was Hansel Gordon Jackson. He came to the Red Deer River Valley in 1903 from Mexico with a train full of Texas longhorns. The ranch's original owner, Lord Delaval James De La Poer Beresford, hired Happy Jack on as a foreman. Beresford, youngest son of a noble British family, died in a train wreck some years later. His black widow, Lady Flo, received a few thousand dollars and a strong suggestion from Lord Beresford's relatives that she forget her titled connections, while Jackson was given the ranch in the badlands.

Happy Jack homesteaded some of the land Beresford had leased, and stayed on here. He ranched, ran the ferry, drank and heaped abuse on the world in general until he died in 1942.

The buildings were close to nowhere. The dry sage shifted in the wind, a few tumbleweeds moved across the flats. The isolation was complete. There were no gentling trees or shrubs, nothing but the disintegrating old ferry road, the collapsing corrals, and the moldering haystacks. Happy Jack must have had the same resources as most of the early settlers in these parts: forebearance, endurance and self-sufficiency. To choose this spot, though, he must also have been a natural loner. The land we saw was dry, and hard to work. The mosquitoes were fierce, the loneliness insistent.

We walked past the buildings and followed the road up onto the prairie. A gas well in the distance was the only indication that this place had been 'civilized' for a hundred years. Teepee rings, stones that once weighted skin walls against the wind, lined the valley edge, undisturbed, in perfect circles. They were covered with orange and green lichen. I counted a dozen where they lay, commanding a view down both arms of a bend in the river.

The wind, the moving river, and the Wolf Coulee Badlands cutting back into the prairie, were spread out in front of us. It was exhilirating to stand alone, to absorb the sight of an area that does not properly involve humans.

There is no shortage of decaying homesteads and ghost towns along this part of the river now, and no shortage of teepee rings, but there aren't many people still living on sites like this one. It isn't as important to be near the water as it once was, and not many choose to live in a badlands valley. Happy Jack was a Georgian who had seen a lot of places before he stopped and stayed across from Wolf Coulee; he must have felt strength and satisfaction in borrowing this place.

April	20 Sun.	Drunk
	21 Mon.	Drunk
	22 Tues.	Drunk
	23 Wed.	Drunk
	24 Thurs.	Red Had a Calf 8 Days over
	25 Fri.	Still Drunk
	26 Sat.	Sick
	27 Sun.	Dam Sick
	28 Mon.	Worse
	29 Tues.	Very Feeble
	30 Wed.	Long Live Booze
		Hurrah for Hell

"Happy Jack" Jackson, 1913

It was early evening when we started down from the prairie into the valley. We followed a little coulee into the badlands, continued on to the bottomland, stopped again at Happy Jack's cabin as darkness was settling. The buildings were all rough log construction, with pole roofs covered in burlap, dirt and a scattering of prickly-pear cactus. The doors all stood open, frozen by dust, inviting us to walk through the small rooms to look at the remains of Happy Jack's life. Brian watched and waited while I catalogued the bits and pieces that were left, the old razor blades and fruit jar rings.

One of the outside doors was fitted with what was once a fine porcelain doorknob. This had been Lord Beresford's room, the Blue Room, his parlour and the display room for his collection of china. On the inside it looked no different from the others. The ceiling was made of unbarked poles, and pictures had been tacked to the walls. A yellowed calendar showed a lake in Scotland. Beside the calendar was one small window covered by a roller blind that shut out a view of bare sage flat leading across sharp-sided gullies to badlands.

The other rooms held hints of order. Calendars hung on most of the walls. Scraps and tatters of newspaper pages remained where Happy Jack had papered them over the ceilings; he subscribed to and read papers from Brooks, Calgary, Montreal, New York and Texas. The walls were lined with fruit crates nailed up as cupboards, and rows of nails for hangers. A worn broom lay on a table.

None of the carpentry was very painstaking. The bunks leaned every which way on mismatched legs. The sleepers, Happy Jack and his crew of itinerant hired men, must have either fought the slope of the bunks or lain huddled in the corners; I suspect they fought.

Not all the old ranchers spent as much time alone as he did, and they didn't all face country that had as little gentleness as the spread he faced, but they all worked hard at imposing their version of sense on a wilderness. Happy Jack resisted everyone who tried to move him out of the valley as he grew older. He kept on planting a garden, riding his horses, raising his oats, running the ferry — and cursing the weather, the world, mosquitoes, William Aberhart and Nellie McClung — until he died. This place was home, but at some time or other he had become tired or frightened enough of the moan of the wind down the narrow breezeway between his rooms, to try and cut it off with a baffle of shingles.

After dark we stood in front of the main cabin. It was quiet. We couldn't even hear the river. We craned our necks back and the sky seemed to flatten out, settle on us. Coyotes back along the valley started barking, first one, then an answer, then a group, snarling and yelping, fighting or playing.

Happy Jack chose a home that must constantly have reminded him of his isolation, yet he must also have found its offerings inexhaustible. The valley here was rich in a way that populated places cannot be, rich in sky and quiet water and empty spaces.

July   9 Wed.   *Not a human left good by*
           18 Fri   *106° Dam the World by sections*
           20 Sun.   *Not a Dam Human Left*
           31 Thurs.   *Good By God Dam It*

"Happy Jack" Jackson, 1941

Deadlodge Canyon

Fragmented dinosaur bone

Shoulder blade of Duckbilled dinosaur

Mexico Ranch

Tool shed

Barbed wire

Work bench, Mexico Ranch

Horseshoe Canyon

This was the moneymaker valley before for miners and still is not bad. Down here cleaner air, river flows by if you want to fish. I like this valley, I don't trade it no place.

Joseph Orosz, retired miner, in conversation, 1981

Brian and I drove toward the Drumheller Valley during the first cold snap of winter. The day was so clear, bright and cold the passing country seemed like an overexposed movie.

We got out of the car to have some lunch and found that the lack of snow said nothing about the temperature. The wind hit us as we stood on the edge of Horseshoe Canyon, so we pulled on mitts and covered our faces. Brian pointed to a bird overhead. I looked up and saw my first bald eagle, gliding by above us without a twitch of its long-fingered wings.

The reindeer moss on the hillsides was still green, the valley dotted with clumps of spruce, but the poplar clumps were nude and skeletal. The tumbleweed was leafless, ready to roll, its edges curling in, the points and corners rounding. Things looked wet. As we walked, we found that the bentonite and sandstone were glazed with ice anywhere the sun had missed.

The view seemed heavy. Bands of dark brown and coal black overwhelmed the lighter shades. We could see a farmhouse on the valley's edge; the strata stacked below it exposed the shallow camouflage of topsoil on which the surrounding ranches and farms depended. Rabbits ambled across the dark hillsides. Somehow they'd missed the fact that there was no snow on the ground, and their white winter coats stood out sharply against the dark earth.

We drove down into the valley at Drumheller, skirted the city, and followed the railroad and the river until we came to Rosedale Creek Coulee. The valley road crosses the creek a dozen times as the water meanders back and forth between the coulee walls. We passed a few houses, each with its t.v. antenna reaching up toward prairie level. The empty spaces between the exposed houses on the chalky flats were their most striking feature.

Many people told us that this part of the valley hadn't always looked this way. Peter Fidler found coal in the area in 1793, and like most explorers, interested in what can be taken away from a new land, he prepared the way for industry. Commercial mining didn't really get rolling until 1912, but from then until the early 1960s, coal had the whole valley from East Coulee to Nacmine jumping. The Rosedeer Mine operated at Wayne, and right through the Depression men pulled down a steady wage in the coulee while up on the prairie the topsoil blew away.

The cash flow brought people, nine or ten thousand to this stretch of the valley alone during the 1930s. Times change. When we pulled up to the Rosedeer Hotel, next to the Wayne General Store and Post Office, the only people around were the bar lady and a couple of little girls. The woman in the tavern admitted that things were a bit quiet for a Saturday afternoon, but then there was a football game on. The store wasn't open, because her boss ran it too, and her boss wasn't there.

She couldn't tell us much about the mining days, but she did say that Wayne's grain elevator had recently burned down, and there didn't seem to be much left for the town. The farmers up on the prairie still dropped in for a beer, she said, and tourists kept the place going in summer, but things were slow. We felt welcome, and she seemed pleased to have someone to talk with.

The valley's edge was beginning to cut off what was left of the early evening sun, so we drove on, through Nacmine and up onto the prairie, heading for Bleriot Ferry. We took our time. Darkness caught up with us, and we were a little lost when I noticed that a huge snowy owl was keeping pace with us on our left. It stayed behind the fan of our headlights and picked up just enough light to glow. It reminded me of the eagle we had seen earlier. Both birds were slow-moving, solitary, purposeful.

When we found an empty campground, we pitched our tent in the dark, then tried to warm up in our sleeping bags. The air smelled sharp and cold. We could hear the rustling grind of ice on the river.

Nine thousand people from the children up to the oldest ones you could count. Little shack here, little shack there. You know how poor was the people. Who has hammer and saw and he knows how to drive the nails in the wood, he builds himself one room and two room house all over, wherever they could hang on by the hill.

Joseph Orosz

When we opened our eyes to the cold morning, our water and food were frozen, so we put off breakfast. We walked to warm ourselves. The ferry had been pulled up out of the water; the ferryman's house stood empty.

We ate some brittle chocolate as we drove out of the valley and turned toward Drumheller. There weren't many people moving this early on the year's first cold Sunday. As we descended again into the valley, the sun was just beginning to catch the ice on the dry yellow grass and stubble. We crossed the river and got out at the old Midland Mine site, across from McMullen Island.

The empty mine office stood along the road, but there wasn't much else to show that this once was a going concern. We walked back away from the road and found bits of coal scattered all over the ground. Cribbing marked the location of some of the old pits. Rusted rails and empty railbeds showed where the cars had hauled away black diamonds.

Drumheller was born a boomtown. The erosion that created the badlands also uncovered seams of coal up to 18 feet thick, and coal like that was irresistible bait in fuel-hungry western Canada in 1912, when Sam Drumheller and a few others took out their mining leases. It was hard to believe that the boom hadn't slowed until after the Second World War. Millions of tons of coal were taken from the valley. Now, all that remained of the mines was a jumble of artifacts, material for archeologists and nostalgists.

We drove up to Rosedale and walked over the suspension bridge where miners used to cross to the Star Mine. The scene was similar: rusted cable, bits and beams of lumber. A half-century of frantic activity — strikes, brawls, petitions to a government that was allowing the industry to die — seemed to have been erased forever.

We might have repeated the experience at mine sites up and down the valley, but our last stope was the Atlas Mine, near Cambria. It had stopped producing just a few years earlier, so the buildings still stood. We wandered through and around them. As we did, hundreds of pigeons burst into the air and resettled just ahead of our path. They spread over the rooftops and flowed through the broken windows.

A man putting up his storm windows across the road was watching us as we prowled around. Both Brian and I expected to be told to move along by a caretaker, so when a truck pulled up behind our car and a man got out and walked toward us, we were prepared to leave gracefully. "Do you guys work here?" he asked. We told him that we did not, and he replied, "Can you tell me anything about it?" He was working in the area maintaining natural gas pipelines, he explained, and thought he'd have a look at the mine site, because he'd never seen it before. He didn't expect it would be around much longer, he said. Judging from the state of the other mines in the valley, we were sure he was right.

The new boom, gas and oil, will never be a part of the valley the way the mines once were. Mines are immobile. They can open and close, and they can decay, but they can't move on like an oil rig. Some of the people we met, especially the oldtimers, were waiting for the oil to dry up. Coal will be waiting when it does, they told us.

Winter time was thirty-five, forty below, up there. Oh, you was glad to get to the slope then, boy. All that nice hot air coming out, and pretty soon you feel snow flake melting off, and you shake it down. When you used to be the real miner, when you used to the system, honest to God you like it.

Joseph Orosz

Rosedeer Hotel, Wayne

Home, Wayne

Home, Nacmine

Munson Badlands

Coal cars near East Coulee

Abandoned mine tipple, Atlas Mine

Snow-covered badlands, Dry Island Buffalo Jump

Farm, Wayne

Josef Orosz at home, Nacmine

Kitchen, Josef Orosz's home

Horsethief Canyon

Pretty soon, if they don't develop that gas and oil business, Drumheller is going to be booming, because lots more coal around here.

Joseph Orosz

We returned in early spring, drove past Munson and dropped down from the greening prairie to Bleriot Ferry while it was still early morning. The crossing had been named after the pioneer brother of the early french aviator, Louis Bleriot; it is a plain spot that must once have been very remote. A scrappy old snack-bar and convenience store hugged a badlands slope on the Munson side of the river. A sign nearby on an old wagon announced that there was a dude ranch not far off.

We waited behind other traffic for several minutes and then were able to cross on the ferry. The ferryman worked automatically. He dragged open the cable barriers, dragged them shut, started the big diesels, crossed the river and then reversed the process at the other side, preserving an endangered route across the Red Deer River. Although the government closed most of the ferries on Alberta's rivers as bridges were built, the ferryman said he doubted that the town of Drumheller would ever let this one go.

We found a campsite in the Department of Transport campground across the river. We were near the bank, shaded by big cottonwoods. After putting up our tent, we set out for a loop around the feature attraction of the area, the Dinosaur Trail. We took our time, stopping at the viewpoints and points of interest along with the other tourists.

A knot of cars looked out over the valley toward Horsethief Canyon across the river. One man sat in his car while his wife and daughter stood and looked. When his patience ran out he revved the engine and honked his horn until his wife bawled him out. Cameras clicked and one man swung his boy toward the edge of the valley; both screamed with laughter.

It really was a beautiful valley. A haze in the air softened the morning light. A bright green flat, sectioned by stream beds, separated the river from the badlands. The colours blended warmly.

Up along the rim of the valley, gas-well sites and rocking horsehead oil pumps stood against the sky. Directly below the viewpoint, perhaps a hundred feet down, lay an old car that had gone over the edge *Rebel-Without-A-Cause* style. The prairie was covered in young wheat.

We drove back down into the valley, crossed on the ferry and headed up to the rim of Horsethief. Family-sized groups were laying out their picnics and shouting at errant sons who were exploring the badlands. Most people seemed to be looking at a bright yellow and blue sign that described the sights.

We continued on into Drumheller to the municipal park next to the river. Drumheller seemed a city like many others in the West, although it showed its age a bit more than most. A few old square business blocks still sat challenging the badlands, even though a spreading city now intervened.

We moved on to the Drumheller Museum. The gift shop and a tourist information counter both sat in the lobby, and the two kept the room busy. The displays inside were fading in places, but the museum was doing a good job of providing an important service. The staff members were pleasant, eager to talk and interested in their subject. A steady flow of people around us were learning a lesson in prehistory.

As we drove east out of town we passed a huddled group of cement dinosaurs in front of a shopping centre. Their style, lots of personality but a little bizarre, matched "Dinny", the *Tyrannosaurus* who stood at the bridge as we entered the city from the north. We drove until we reached the East Coulee hoodoos. A crowd of people stood in the parking lot across the road, while others walked through the hoodoos on well-worn paths. The formations were too striking to ignore.

When we backtracked and branched off to Horseshoe Canyon, we found another Chamber of Commerce sign, bright blue and yellow. A bearded man in the parking lot was running a fossil concession. He had an assortment of bone and shell bits and a few big carnivore teeth that he was hawking to the curious. I asked him the price on one of the best preserved teeth, and he replied, "I wouldn't want to part with this."

"Are you sure?" asked Brian, sensing a sales pitch.

"Not unless the price was right," he answered. He had located his business well; the canyon spread out behind him, an astoundingly deep and colourful basin.

We drove back to Drumheller to complete our loop, and dropped in on "Prehistoric Parks." This enclosure of badlands, dotted with more cement dinosaurs, was commanded by a pedestalled pterodactyl. A stegosaurus followed a low trail, and a gentle, enormous cement Christ stood with arms outstretched, blessing his scaly flock. Judging from the crowds, it seemed quite a popular place.

We made one final stop at Drumheller's famous little church, the sanctuary that has seated "twenty thousand, six at a time." Again a sign described the spectacle for us. Behaviour should be reserved, it cautioned. This was not a tourist attraction, we were told, but rather a place of meditation.

We sat against the car and talked about the valley. What we had seen was full of contrasts: pleasantly helpful people and people who treated tourism as a medicine show; beautiful and accessible badlands that people were avoiding, and plain-looking spots that were overrun; careful, responsible interpretation of the valley and crass commercial exploitation.

The day as a whole, though, had been positive; we'd seen some extraordinary things.

We rolled back over the ferry to our camp as darkness came on. We walked along the river toward the sound of a party, stood in the darkness watching cars grind over the sage flat, then abandoned the evening for bed.

It had been a hectic day in which we had been constantly pressing through people who were looking at or for the same things we were. We had faced brightly obtrusive signs and cement dinosaurs at every turn, yet the place still felt more remarkable than irritating. Most southern Albertans face their badlands with a great deal of disinterest; some find them significant only because they hinder ranching. In Drumheller however everyone does seem to acknowledge the landscape. Sometimes the acknowledgement may seem inappropriate, but it is an acknowledgement nonetheless.

So after when they take you to the room, if there's any more money in the pocket, the girl take it out. And the poor miner, when they coming out, wobbling here, wobbling there, scratching his head next morning and he says, "Oh, my stomach." Can't even buy a box of chew, no money left. Where did all the money go? Left it in the whorehouse.

Joseph Orosz

We crawled out of our sleeping bags at about 7:30 the next morning because we had a breakfast date. A camper had pulled into our parking spot near Bleriot Ferry the night before, and the people in it had offered us some bacon and eggs. The spring day was already warm. We were sluggish after having been kept awake by a motorbikers' party until four in the morning, when the liquor finally ran out and a thunderstorm chased the boys inside.

The camper held a local lady and her friend. The lady's name was Nellie, and as she set out the food she opened a converation. She wanted to talk about cults and evil. "There's good," she said, "and there's evil, and that's all there is to it."

"That might be so," I said, "but the trouble sometimes is telling the difference."

"The difference," returned Nellie, a little offended, "is obvious."

Paul, her friend, finally spoke. He hadn't said much but "good morning" so far. "Oh, I wouldn't go that far," he said, then lapsed back into silence. Nellie was not a forceless woman, so we found his comment courageous. It pulled her up short, and the chat turned quickly to another topic.

Paul sat quietly. His hands were lumpy with arthritis and his cheeks were covered in a tangle of exploded capillaries. He wore a farmer's body, a record of hard work and forebearance.

We excused ourselves and set off for another day along the Drumheller Valley. The stretch of river just upstream and downstream from Drumheller is the most settled part of the badlands. The natural features are magnificent, but the people along the river are a worthy distraction. The towns between Nacmine and East Coulee were born in the mining boom. While there isn't much left of these places, the remaining residents still talk about their communities with an enthusiasm that suggests they might be on the brink of another boom. They also express a patience and a sense of home that suggests that it won't really matter whether the boom comes or not.

We stopped in at the hotel in Nacmine for a beer. The tavern was surprisingly empty for a summer Saturday afternoon. We took a little round table across from the juke box and were waited on by a sober-looking woman. As soon as we sat down, a short, heavy man in work clothes bumped up to the table and asked where Danny was. I told him we didn't know where Danny was, which he took as an invitation to sit down. "You call Danny over here," he told me.

"I don't know Danny," I told him.

"Aw, you're chicken," he said. Then he turned to Brian: "And you're honest." He thought this one over for a bit. "You're chicken, and you're honest." This was worth passing on, so he called Danny himself over from the pool table. "Hey Danny," he said, "this guy says you're chicken, and this guy says you're honest." Danny looked at us and grinned an alcoholic grin.

"You're both right," he said. "I'm chicken and I'm honest."

He propped himself up with his pool cue and laughed like mad. Time for another beer all around.

We walked out into the quiet town, past a few housing starts along the river, a lot of older homes, and an imposing, dormant mine; a pile of waste coal smoldered.

We drove up through Drumheller, stopping to talk to a hotel owner on the outskirts. "It's a city like any city," he told us. "Sometimes it's easy to make money and sometimes it's harder. But you can't beat the climate," he said, "and it's a great place for tourists."

Further down the valley, just outside of Drumheller, we stopped and picked up a hitchiker, a young man on his way home to Cambria, a small cluster of houses huddled on alkali against badlands exposures on the valley wall. "How do you like it?" I asked him.

"It's home."

Brian this time: "Are you going to stay?"

"You don't leave the place where you're born and raised," he answered.

There was a pause, and Brian asked, "Do you like it, living here? There's no place you want to go?"

"Yeah," he said, "this place suits me. I don't bother nobody and nobody bothers me." This was obviously our cue to stop bothering him.

Nacmine Hotel and Mike's Tavern

Life-size model of Tyrannosaurus Rex, Drumheller

Life-size model of Protoceratops, Prehistoric Parks, Newcastle

Storefront, Nacmine

Prospects

There is nothing that does not leave its effect. We study the accumulated remains.

William Dawe in Badlands by Robert Kroetsch

Moonrise, Deadlodge Canyon Badlands

Petroglyphs

The rains of ages have laid bare
The ancient dead

From "A Story of the Past," Charles H. Sternberg, 1911

Except for the cool nights, early summer feels like mid-summer along the Milk River. We turned onto the road to Writing-on-Stone at noon. Dust filled the air as cars packed with families in cowboy hats drove toward the park. A sign announced the Milk River Rodeo; we hadn't arrived on a quiet weekend.

We camped in a nice stand of cottonwoods, but even in the shade the heat was almost unbearable. We decided to siesta. The sky was a clear, washed-out blue. On the ground, nothing moved except the cowboys. Rodeos seem to thrive on heat, dust and cold beer.

After sweating away part of the afternoon in our tents, we went down the valley to see the petroglyphs that give the park its name. A petroglyph is a rock-picture. The hard, rounded hoodoos and flat perpendicular sandstone walls of this valley served as the medium for the ritual art of successive tribes of Indians over hundreds of years. The Shoshoni, Blackfoot, Gros Ventres and Peigans all carved in the rock at Writing-on-Stone.

We followed a trail at the base of the cliffs. All of the flat surfaces were defaced with graffitti, some of them dated before the turn of the century. The graffitti, like the petroglyphs, had survived the eroding rain on these smooth, slightly-retreating rock faces.

Writing-on-Stone cannot really be called proper badlands. Instead of being patterned by the raw erosive cutting of sediments, its valley walls are smooth, solid faces, interrupted by durable-looking columns and grassy slopes. It shares many badlands features, such as hoodoos and the river habitat, but it seems more controlled, more refined. The petroglyphs are part of this control; they record the involvement of man along the river.

Rock-pictures have sacred significance. They are said to have been carved by spirits in darkness in order to tell the future to those who could read them. Their defacement — the scratched autographs of picnickers — is criminal, but we couldn't help spending as much time reading the signatures and love notes as tracing the stylized men and animals. The names were layered over the pictographs like valley sediments; the carvings on top were the most accessible.

Not far away, within hearing range, the rodeo was in full swing. Teepees were set up, the parking lot was filled with campers and motor-homes, a loud-speaker was croaking out events and winners, and stetsons were waving. A fat yellow marmot crawled out of the rock ahead of us, sat on a flat slab, and whistled. Below, a green flat led down to the river. The valley was shallow and sharp-sided. The hoodoos, smooth-edged, looping and rounded, rose suddenly from the plane of the valley floor.

Just ahead of us, commanding the mouth of Police Coulee, stood a reconstructed North West Mounted Police post. The original had been placed there in 1887. Puny and lonely, it sat in this strange valley, on guard against rustlers and whiskey-runners who used the shelter of the coulees to cross the international border. The men must have thrown themselves with a vengeance into the job of protecting the Queen's territory from the malevolent influences seeping northward from the Republic, or they might have lost their sense of civilization in this beautiful, frightening place. They carved their names in the valley wall across the river: more spirit-writing.

We caught up with a park naturalist who spun out the story of the vision quests which the natives were assumed to have carried out in this valley. The significance of the petroglyphs, he told us, was often known to the artist alone; the naturalist knew as little about them as we did. He pointed out the narrow slots carved in the rock by the rubbing of arrowheads, apparently to confer power on a warrior or hunter. It was easy to believe that these walls — seemingly carved by a sweeping, conscious hand — had or have intrinsic spiritual importance.

The rodeo, the N.W.M.P. post, the native record and the other tourists should have made the valley seem busy, but we felt comfortably alone. Worldless natural forms rose and surrounded us. The terrain was too powerful to be much disturbed by human activity.

Animals come on the stage of life, exist for a greater or lesser period as it may happen, and then disappear; and the old saw "That every dog has his day" is as literally true of the past as of the present.

Charles H. Sternberg

We turned back to our campsite for dinner just as the rodeo was winding down. Cowboys and spectators streamed into the campground looking for picnic tables. A sprinkler truck came by, dampening the road to settle the dust, but car after car stirred the grit up again in clouds. Feet in pointed boots trampled the grass that grew in carefully watered plots. Our every movement seemed to mock the groundskeepers' efforts to fight the dryness.

The heat pressed on into the evening, but we were feeling lazily adventurous and well-fed. As the light began to fail, we strolled down a trail to the flat. Sage and mosquitoes assaulted us with smell and sound. We walked along with our flashlights on the rock face, trying to find a petroglyph we'd been told of that afternoon.

We eventually found the picture, faint but complete, still and violent. It showed a battle scene. In late summer, 1866, a party of Peigans attacked a party of Gros Ventres, Crows and Cree in revenge for the killing of their chief. The camp, the rings of teepees, the horses, the bows and arrows and the guns were all shown. Bullets streaked across the picture as dotted lines. Lynn played a flashlight along one of the trajectories until it pierced a man in close combat with another. We traced the scene across the cliff face; death after death was memorialized in the smooth, slowly weathering rock.

We climbed to the lip of the valley for a last sight of the sun. The view from the prairie was spectacular, dominated by the sharp gold of the dry prairie grass as it reflected the light of the setting sun. Marna led the way back down to the flat. In the dusk near the graffitti-covered rock-pictures, two pretty young girls passed us; small black caps covered the knot of hair on each of their heads. Behind them came a stern-looking young man who stopped at a pump by the trail and pumped water over the hands of an equally stern-looking young woman. An even more severe older couple followed, dressed sombrely in black. They looked at us cautiously. All carried black books, either hymnals or Bibles. I offered a good evening, which they accepted very cordially; they smiled. We were intruding on the end of an evening service.

We climbed away and sat in the hoodoos to listen to the night noises and smell the night smells. An owl was calling — an even, slow hoot — and behind the sound of the owl was an even lower voice, the thud of a ruffed grouse. During the slow heat of this day, the rodeo, campers and guided tours had rattled on, but now the pace had eased.

The Mounted Police outpost sat in silhouette across the flat. The Sweetgrass Hills stood purple and solid across the border. The day and the place demanded reflection. The frogs were gulping, and soon it became cool enough to send us back to the warmth of our camp.

A river of stars flowed on the blue night, gave edge to the valley's walls.

Robert Kroetsch, Badlands

Writing-on-Stone and Sweetgrass Hills

Glacial erratic

Sandstone pillars

Coulee wall

Great horned owl

Fall colours, Red Deer River

"The wisdom of man is foolishness to God." How could it be otherwise.

Charles H. Sternberg

We unloaded the canoe at the Emerson Bridge on the Red Deer River on a cloudless, hot day. The plan was for me to wait with the gear at the bridge while Brian drove down-river to Jenner Ferry, left the car and caught a ride back with Sid Andrews.

After filling our water jugs, I slid the canoe into about four inches of water. Mud formed the banks, fine and gluey in some spots, sandy in others; it stuck to my feet the way dough sticks to your fingers. As I pulled the boat past the bridge pilons to deeper water, I stepped into quickmud and was suddenly fighting to get my feet back. It wasn't a dangerous feeling, but it was a little uncomfortable. Each time I tried to lift one foot, the other sank in more deeply. I finally lay back on a drier part of the bank, grabbed each leg under the knee and pulled myself out.

With our gear aboard, the canoe was ready for Brian's return, so I decided to have a look around. The valley was lined with cottonwoods. The river, silty and dark, slipped between treed banks. Across the water, grassy slopes led up to the prairie, and behind me were badlands. From the riverbank, it was hard to imagine the level world just over the valley rim.

Trucks were my only company. I could hear them coming from a long way off: big trucks, stock trucks, oil tankers, moving vans and big freighter rigs. Sound would grow very gradually, then suddenly the truck would roar down into the valley, flash by and grind up the other side. I walked out onto the bridge and looked down into the water to find the deepest channel. The river was low, as it always is in summer, and all along its length were sandbars and shallows. I could see the channel as a dark, snaking path under the lighter surface of the river; it hugged the outside bank on the bends, crossed over and hugged the next bank down along the river as far as I could see. There was plenty of water to float us, but the trick would be to follow the river *beneath* the river.

When the waiting began to get to me, I walked up the highway to the prairie. I saw lots of dry, brown grass and two pronghorn antelope that tossed their white rumps in my direction and bounded off as soon as they caught sight of me. Empty sky, empty country, empty road; at least that's the way it looked from where I stood.

Brian finally rolled into the campground as the valley was sliding into evening. He and Sid hadn't connected on time, and rather than relaxing through the sunny day, Brian and I had both sweated it out and counted the hours. It would have been better to have left our watches in the city.

A few neighbours, most of them welders working on pipelines or rigs, drove in and set up in the campground. A black Labrador came out of one of the trucks and mooched around us as we ate dinner; she waited patiently for a lick of this or that, steadily and energetically wagging her tail.

When we started up into the hills right after dinner, the dog came with us. The slope we climbed was grassy, stable and covered in prickly-pear cactus. Since we wanted to relax more than we wanted to hike, we picked a high, level spot on the hill and sat looking down toward the river. A dog barked below us somewhere in the cottonwoods. Our Lab listened. The sage was strong in the air; a little breeze carried it past us. It was suddenly quite cool, and the mosquitoes retired as the stars appeared and shone. Geese were settling in on a sandbar in the river; a ragged series of honks filtered up to us. An owl called, and the dog pricked up her ears again. I tried to take in everything around me: the rough, bristly, brittle feel of the grass beneath us; the cold, smooth touch of the light wind; the patterns of the stars; the smell of the sage; the sound of the geese; the dog's company. There was too much to sort out as the evening unlocked.

The hard side of the badlands, the side that dealt us heat, fatigue and isolation, is almost always tempered with insight; badlands are a place for testing, for pondering. This day had been unpleasant, unprovocative and tedious, because we'd tried to put the valley on schedule. The evening, watched with a little less attention to discomfort, had given us a chance to find what we'd missed.

South and east they drifted. On their port side long stretches of prairie sloped undulating and ocean-green, under the white and exploded puffs of cumulus cloud, sloped and fell from the horizon to the water's edge; on their starboard, under the blue outline of the Wintering Hills, the low buttes were humped far back from the water, across a flood plain where ranchers ran cattle.

Robert Kroetsch, Badlands

By the time we had reloaded the canoe, it was daylight. There was not a whisp, not a puff, not a fragment of cloud in the sky. We pushed the canoe sideways into the deep water and got in. I stuck my feet over the side and rubbed the pasty mud off my soles.

We were off down the river, crossing from side to side, watching the cutbanks, trying to guess the channel. We washed by the rolling yellow hills. Silly black coots scooted across in front of the canoe as we passed their spots on the bank. Kingbirds, brown with sharply defined black and white spotted tails, flapped out of the trees killed by the high water of a spring thaw.

On some stretches, we followed a gentle bank, grassy or thick with willows, littered with deadwood showing the marks of beavers' teeth. Along one of these banks we suddenly noticed that we were passing a coyote. It was tawny, yellow-brown and sleek, with long bright fur. We were very near before it noticed us. When it did see us coming, it watched for a while instead of running. We were almost abreast of it — an arm's length away — when it turned its head, still looking at us, and grabbed a mouthful of grass. It tore out the mouthful with a twist of its long, thin face, and backed up the bank.

We slipped suddenly into the Steveville Badlands. They rose up around us almost as abruptly as badlands fall away from the prairie. We passed muskrats and mule deer along the bank of a long island, paddled around the tip of a sandbar and reversed our course into a backwater.

We stopped against a steep bank and struggled up it, through the scrub margin. Just beyond us were cottonwoods that curtained off the valley wall. The hills in the distance were carved, lined with hoodoos, tall, dominating.

In the evening, as the light softened, we crossed a withered mud flat marked with deer tracks, then walked through the sage past rank upon rank of hoodoos. Crossing a white, windswept alkali flat, we came on some old farm machinery, neatly arranged and sinking. Four or five inches of the wheels of a disk harrow and a seeder were hidden by the arid, pale dust. Someone must once have plowed the flat, but the equipment was now more out of place than it would have been on a city street.

The hills rose around us, deep and rounded, grey-brown, reddened and glowing in the dusk. Surrounded by the Steveville Badlands, we climbed up and up, found a ridge and followed it to grazing land. The nighthawks were sounding, but the prairie remained a quiet place. We turned our backs on the empty expanse that showed not even a ranch house light in the distance or a flash of headlights on a hidden road. We watched the valley become a labyrinth of shadow.

We found our way back down to our tents hidden in the dark behind the screen of cottonwoods and willows, and made tea. The mosquitoes were gone; the bats were out. We put our backs against the ground and watched the sky. It was a clear night; we saw a steady trickle of falling stars and a sectioning of the sky by criss-crossing satellites.

A noisy bunch of geese picked our spot on the river to spend the night, so in the interest of a peaceful, quiet sleep, we went down to scare them off. They didn't care. We shouted and threw branches, but they didn't even honk louder.

As we cleaned up, an owl beat toward us with its slow wings and settled in a dead, barkless luminously white cottonwood. It made a strange burbling screech several times and then took up hooting respectably. It was a Great horned owl; there was no mistaking its silhouette against the moonless sky, dark upon dark in the angular, bony tree. Its call was low, steady and unanswered.

The next morning, we pressed through a dense border of thorny buffaloberry on the river's south bank. The brush reached well above our heads. The paths through it had been made by mule deer and were overgrown four-and-a-half feet from the ground.

We stepped out of this tangle onto a grassy plateau that was cut into small sections by raw-sided runoff gullies and bordered by badlands hills. Rounded mounds of bentonitic clay, lined with yellowish, pencil-thin streaks in an alligator-skin pattern, capped most of the hills.

We found crumbled fossil bone along the bases of some hills. At two spots, after tracing a trail of bone, we found long, badly deteriorated skeletons weathering out of the sediments near the hilltops.

Brian led us straight to a hill dotted over with large fossil limb bones. They were lying on the surface, fractured but not scattered, covered with a mottled pattern of white-orange lichen. Nearby, eroding out from the same material, were two fossil logs. They were red and cream, fractured into pieces like thick slices of a loaf, their rings and grain still distinct. Both the remains of the dinosaurs and the remains of their lush environment lay neatly displayed on the dry hillside. Brian was in his element among the fossils, so I left him to them and went off alone.

I walked to the edge of a deep, precipitous valley. The comfortable morning had become a blisteringly hot noon. My skin was already sunburned, and I could feel it getting worse. I listened: nothing but the wind. The chirps and whistles of starlings, sparrows and warblers had ceased; the heat was too much for them. I looked to the north. The badlands were dominated by a pallisade of tall, flat-sided sandstone hills that rose from a high table of land. They were smooth and distinct, sharp and stark, even in comparison with this austere landscape. Tilting lines of shifting sediment — umber and auburn on a background of bone-grey — striated their sides. A jackrabbit skittered across the washout below me.

I looked away and saw a cricket, a near-invisible brown spot as it sat unmoving on a rock. I tossed pebbles at it and tried to think cool thoughts. The cricket may have felt that the falling rocks were a danger not worth running from, or it may simply have relied on its colour camouflage to keep it from all possible harm. It seemed irritatingly indifferent to my presence whether I was throwing things at it or not.

When Brian finally came looking for me, the cricket sat surrounded by heaps of pebbles, exactly as it had been sitting all along. Brian watched me for a moment, then nudged the cricket with his toe. It reluctantly hopped off, its wings a startling pattern of orange and black when finally spread.

The day had been hot and sultry; as I came upon a coal miners tunnel . . . , I found relief by going in some distance. The floor was deeply covered with fine dust, making a restful place; and it is little wonder I fell asleep; I never knew how long I slept, but when I awoke, I was overpowered with surprise, I could not tell whether I had awakened in eternity, or Time had turned back his dial, and carried me back to the old Cretaceous Ocean. At all events however, I found myself lying under a great red-wood tree. Stretching before me to the south as far as the eyes could reach, a mighty ocean lay as level as a thrashers' floor to the distant horizon, while to the north an interminable forest on the low-lands . . . .

Charles H. Sternberg

Badlands, ironstone, Deadlodge Canyon

Wash sands on ironstone

Lichens

Gas well

Evening, Steveville Badlands

Canada geese

Tolman Badlands

Eroded sandstone

Sandstone rills

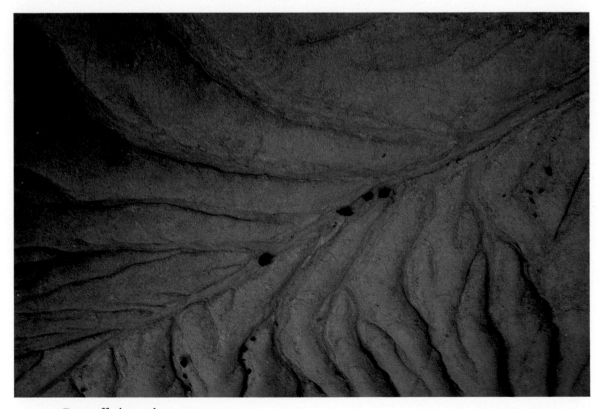

Run-off channel

Sandhill Creek and Deadlodge Canyon

Juniper root

Greasewood on sandstone pediment

The river, there, as brown as the surrounding buttes; the brown river bleached pale in the light and not so darkly stained as the long sandbars that swam up out of the falling water; the sandbars wave-marked and flat too, bird-tracked, the birds gone; the river wide there, shallow.

Robert Kroetsch, Badlands

The hills on the south side of the river near Steveville were so dense and diverse that a great deal of the world seemed to be packed into a very small area. We chose the tallest hill we could see and climbed it to take in the view.

The hill narrowed as we climbed; at the top there was room for only one of us. Brian struggled up to the tiny pinnacle with his camera and tripod. A strong wind was blowing, and the first time Brian let go of the camera, the tripod toppled over. He caught the stand just as the camera smacked into the hillside.

When he deciced to come down, I asked him if he wanted to hand down the camera so that he could control his descent. "No," he said, starting to slide, and then, "Catch me!" Our injuries were minor.

Once back at the river, we decided to get rid of some of our grime: sweat that had stacked up in layers, mixed with insect repellant and the distillation of half a salami each. The wind blew along the cold river. Three soapings and a shampoo later we smelled sweet again. It felt like the soft life.

We paddled against the wind as the river curled around the bow of our canoe. Waves moved upstream faster than the summer current flowed downstream. We were working hard, cloths tied around our faces against the reflected sun, when we came upon three old men fishing from the bank. They looked at us a bit incredulously as we paddled past them, until Brian yelled, "Is this the right way to Saskatchewan?"

They seemed tickled, and one by one they shouted back that it was indeed the right way. The last one added, "Is this the way you have fun?" We grinned and didn't answer, which was the only simple way to handle the question.

Badlands challenge an observer, whether he's climbing in the sun, or just trying to sort out what he sees. Shapes and colours are complex and concentrated; the geological and fossil records are presented in clear and intriguing, though esoteric, shorthand. Seeing and reading the record is as much a physical task as a mental one. We *were* enjoying ourselves, but at the price of effort.

In late afternoon we stopped at a stand of cottonwoods and climbed to the prairie through badlands. We walked along the rim, counting teepee rings, then followed a little draw down into the valley. The gully was almost lush; black-eyed susans and wild sunflowers glowed in the lowering light. Tumbleweed had collected around them, enough tumbleweed to swim in.

A deer-path led us into an area that was startlingly barren, paved by a pediment that glared white, harsh and hot. The place appeared destroyed, devastated; rocks were shattered and scattered by erosion. A single starling flitted about. It looked not so much a part of the living valley, this little basin, as an angry abstraction, yet a few yards further on we were again looking out over green cottonwoods.

With no energy left for anything but the river, we pushed off and watched the badlands slide away. Soon yellow rock was poking through the soft sedimentary layers of the Oldman formation. Signs of beaver lined the river. Mature cottonwoods thirty feet high stood girdled and dying along the water's edge. Sweepers lay out over the river with chewed branches two feet above the water level, where beaver had fed in spring at high-water. Reading the deep water on this slow-moving, shallow stretch of river taxed our modest skills as canoists. Each time we ground to a halt on a sandbar, fatigue would settle on us as we climbed out of the canoe and unhappily dragged it across the river bottom.

With most of the trip behind us, we were starting to sing the blues. For the investment of some mental attention and physical effort, we'd had a more than profitable return: complete peace and quiet, a magnificent display of history, an uncluttered display of living things and a uniquely beautiful landscape. It was easy to acquire a taste for this sort of exhaustion.

As we paddled along, kingfishers kept us company. One stayed with us for miles, looking like a stocky bluejay. It flew ahead a few hundred yards, waited for us to catch up, then flew ahead again. It led us out of the badlands before doubling back.

There is such a thing as breathing life into the skeletons that have been buried out of sight these three million years or more.

Charles H. Sternberg

We returned to Deadlodge Canyon by car. At 2:30 in the morning, the valley of the Red Deer opened below the prairie in total darkness. The only noises we heard as we got settled were campers, rustling around in irritation at the disturbance we were causing. Birds started singing just as we crawled into our bags.

Within a few hours, the campground was noisy with people who'd come to see the dedication of Dinosaur Provincial Park as a UNESCO World Heritage Site. We roused ourselves and crawled out of our sleeping bags to have breakfast with the mosquitoes. They bit everthing in the cool of the morning. The lobes of my ears were bitten, the palms of my hands, even my lips.

The ceremony was to be on the edge of the prairie, overlooking the sprawling, pockmarked badlands. The others drove on ahead while I walked up the freshly oiled road. The sky was a clear, hot blue, and except for a line of clouds forming to the south, empty. The road oil smell, heavy and odd in the still air, overwhelmed the sage and dust, absorbed sunlight and belched it back out in indistinct waves of heat.

I was trudging along without much spring in my step when the movement of a mule deer took my eyes to the badlands at the side of the road. In the indirect morning light, the iron colours were richer than they would be by mid-day. The deer ambled unconcernedly along a hillside, while a photographer struggled up a rilled hill with his camera, racing against the disappearance of the animal. Men with television cameras and two separate film crews waited on the valley's edge.

When I reached the prairie, I found, by badlands standards, an immense crowd of people: perhaps 400. The V.I.P.'s were being decked out in complimentary stetsons by smiling hostesses, while the rest of us were treated to lapel buttons and bumper stickers. The flags of the United Nations, Canada and Alberta flew behind a speakers' platform on the valley edge. The occasion called for something short and stirring — something that would tear eyes from the ceremony and fix them on the landscape that lay spread in motley morning reds and browns behind the stage — but a row of chairs on the platform forewarned of a long series of official addresses.

The promise of endless speeches held true. We stood and listened and grew hotter as the morning wore on. A man stood just in front of me with his feet together, eyes on the badlands, ears to the stage, not moving exept to nod his head in intense agreement every so often. He stood straight and attentive while the rest of us steadily sagged.

As the words dragged on, the hills changed, shifting through shadow to a hot glare, broadening and flattening as highlights disappeared under the sun. The program proceeded without inspiration, skirting the subject of the land, until a man from Pakistan, representing the UNESCO Secretariat, stood and spoke with unselfconscious eloquence about the past, and the record of the past that lay in the hills beyond the speakers' stand. The subject shifted suddenly from political benediction to the place itself, and the crowd rejoined the ceremony.

The proceedings ended, and we went directly from the unveiling of the plaque to a free lunch. The clouds that had marshalled in the south finally straggled up to give the odd moment of shade as they drifted across the sun. Helicopters came and went, carrying the V.I.P.'s out over the badlands for a cool, odour-free look.

We walked past the helicopter pad, a makeshift square on the prairie marked off by oil drums and polypropylene rope, then climbed down into badlands. We scrambled across the steep hillsides, away from the road, into the park. Within a few steps we were very much alone.

The river washed by in the distance, and a mule deer walked by just below us. Judging by its phlegmatic step, it may have been the same one I had seen in the morning. With the helicopter gone, the spot was quiet and calm; the view of the valley lay open for enjoyment, undescribed and undedicated. We were sheltered from the fuss up on the prairie, the fuss that obscured the place itself.

We returned to the official event, and found ourselves inside a roped-off rectangle. The bar and the dinner were free, so we couldn't find any convincing reason to leave. We sat with the others in the shade of a semi-trailer. The group, circled like a wagon-train, protected its celebration from the surrounding country, shutting out the reason for the party.

The assemblage drooped under the weight of the food and the heat, but we had still to face another string of speeches. People were thanked, the food was praised, government programs were unfolded. Just when the valley seemed permanently exiled from the occasion, the man from UNESCO again retrieved it and set it before the crowd.

He stood up, said a few words in Urdu, smiled, then translated: "Where is paradise on earth?" he asked, opening his arms to the badlands. "It is here, it is here, it is here."

The still blade of light came over the rimrock; the light grew from purple to a blue veil, from blue to red to orange; the tall and starkly outlined buttes emerged from the darkness. The buttes came as pyramids against the light; they came as mounds, as beehives, as cones. They had those forms of the past . . . .

Robert Kroetsch, Badlands

Badlands near Steveville

Badlands butte, Steveville

Dragonwort and Rubberweed, Valley of the Moon